D1542598

This book belongs to:

THE WORLD'S FUNNIEST DAD!

What did the drummer call his twin daughters?

Anna one, Anna two!

What's black and white and goes around and around?

A penguin in a revolving door.

What time did the man go to the dentist?

Tooth hurt-y.

When does a joke become a dad joke?

When it becomes apparent.

After dinner, my wife asked if I could clear the table.

I needed a running start, but I made it!

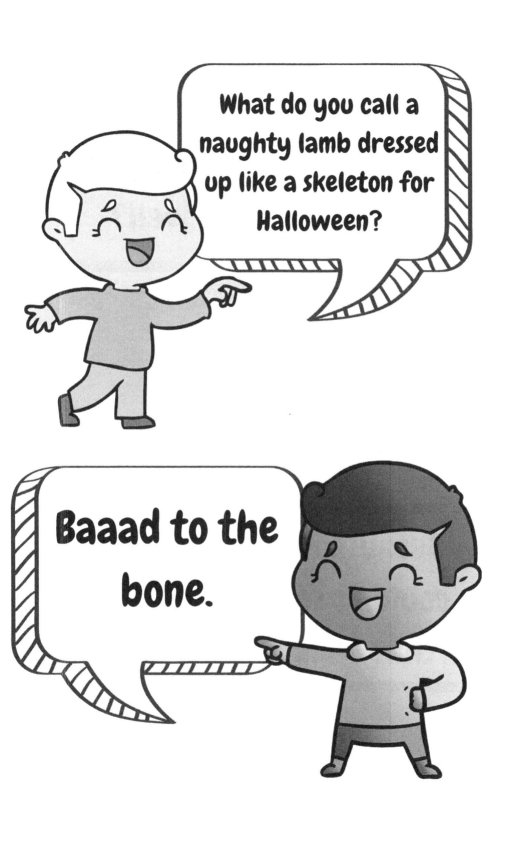

I've been thinking about taking up meditation.

I figure it's better than sitting around doing nothing.

I lost my job at the bank on my first day.

A woman asked me to check her balance, so I pushed her over.

What did the juicer say to the orange during self-quarantine?

Can't wait to squeeze you!

My son asked me to put his shoes on,

but I don't think they'll fit me.

What do sprinters eat before a race?

Nothing— they fast.

I built an electric fence around my garden.

My neighbour is dead against it.

I used to work in a shoe recycling shop.

It was sole destroying.

What do you call a shoe made of a banana?

A Slipper.

Some mornings I wake up grumpy,

on others I let her sleep in.

I spent $100 on a new belt that didn't even fit

My wife said it was a huge waist.

What is the least spoken language in the world?

Sign language.

Son: "How much do all of our bones weigh?"

Dad: "A Skele-ton."

To the person who stole my glasses.

I will find you, I have contacts.

My dog used to chase people on a bike a lot.

It got so bad, finally I had to take his bike away.

A woman walks into a library and asked if they had any books about paranoia.

The librarian says "They're right behind you!"

Made in the USA
Monee, IL
17 June 2022

98168418R00056